STOP
BLEEDING CASH

THE SIX WAYS PEOPLE LOSE MONEY
WITHOUT EVEN KNOWING IT...
AND HOW TO STOP THE BLEEDING

For more information, contact:
Barry Waxler • Universal Financial Publishing • www.barrywaxler.com

ISBNs:
Hardcover: 978-0-692-44708-6
Paperback: 978-0-692-44709-3
eBook: 978-0-692-44710-9

Library of Congress Control Number: 2015907527

Disclaimer: The Publisher and the Author do not guarantee that anyone following the techniques, suggestions, tips, ideas or strategies will become successful. The advice and strategies contained herein may not be suitable for every situation. The Publisher and Author shall have neither liability nor responsibility to anyone with respect to any loss or damage caused, or alleged to be caused, directly or indirectly by the information in this book. Any citations or a potential source of information from other organizations or websites given herein does not mean that the Author or Publisher endorses the information/content the website or organization provides or the recommendations it may make. It is the readers' responsibility to do their own due diligence when researching information. Also, websites listed or referenced herein may have changed or disappeared from the time that this work was created and the time that it is read.

Interior design by Chad McClung

Contents

Disclosure

Barry Waxler is a licensed securities representative and sells securities through Securities America, Inc., Member FINRA/SIPC. Barry Waxler is an investment advisory representative and sells investment advisory services through Verus Capital Partners, LLC. Barry Waxler is a licensed insurance agent and sells insurance products through Universal Financial Consultants, LLC (CA Insurance license #0696653). Verus Capital Partners, Universal Financial Consultants and Securities America are independent, unaffiliated companies.

Apart from fees charged for managing client assets and the commissions earned on securities transactions and/or insurance policy sales, Barry Waxler does not receive referral fees or other compensation from unaffiliated third-party service providers that he may recommend for implementing various investment strategies.

Additional information about Mr. Waxler's investment experience, outside business activities, and regulatory disclosures can be found through FINRA BrokerCheck at www.finra.org. As well, it is important to review Mr. Waxler's Form ADV 2B.

The opinions and forecasts expressed are those of the author, and may not actually come to pass. This information is subject to change at any time based on market and other conditions, and should not be construed as a recommendation of any specific security or investment plan. Past performance does not guarantee future results.

All investments involve the risk of potential investment losses, and no strategy can ensure a profit. Investment strategies may be subject to various types of risk including, but not limited to, market risk, credit risk, interest rate risk, and inflation risk.

Representatives of Securities America do not provide tax or legal advice. Tax law is subject to frequent changes; therefore, it is important to coordinate with your tax advisor. Any tax or legal information provided here is merely an example of current tax regulations with respect to a specific situation, and is not exhaustive.

Annuity products, which are discussed in this material, are long-term investments with surrender penalties for early withdrawal. Withdrawals of taxable amounts are subject to income tax and if taken prior to age 59½ may be subject to a 10% federal tax penalty. Withdrawals will reduce the living benefits, death benefits, and account values. Early withdrawals may be subject to withdrawal charges. An investment in the securities underlying a variable annuity involves investment risk, including possible loss of principal. The contract, when redeemed, may be worth more or less than the original investment. Guarantees are backed by the claims-paying ability of the issuer.

Variable annuities are sold by prospectus only. Investors should carefully consider objectives, risks, charges, and expenses carefully before investing. The contract prospectus and the underlying fund prospectus contain this and other important information. Investors should read the prospectus carefully before investing. For a copy of the prospectus contact your financial advisor.

Of course, tax-qualified contracts such as an IRA, 401(k), etc. are tax-deferred regardless of whether or not they are funded with an annuity. However, annuities do provide other features and benefits including, but not limited to, a guaranteed death benefit and income options, for which a mortality and expense risk fee is charged. You should discuss this decision with your financial advisor.

Foreword

I first met Barry Waxler in 1992 on a racing sailboat in San Diego, and we've been friends ever since. There is something unique about sailing on a thirty-four-foot boat in a race. You get to learn quickly about your fellow crewmembers' personalities and character. Barry has worked with me and my family in financial affairs, and I invited him to be on the community board of directors of the Disabled Businesspersons' Association (DBA) charity, a position he accepted.

When Barry told me he was working on a new financial book, I told him that I would be most interested in reviewing it to find out where his thoughts were going in the money arena—especially since we were just then beginning to come out of the recession. It wasn't long afterward that I received a first draft of Stop Bleeding Cash.

Now, if you're anything like me (always busy), you feel you're pretty savvy about financial matters, especially concerning where your cash is going. And I felt that if there were any "bleeding" of cash in my own financial affairs, I would have surely caught it and stopped it right away. Besides, reading yet another book about something I was sure I already knew seemed to me like drainage of my valuable time. But Barry is a friend, and I had already offered to review his work. I sat down one evening and read Stop Bleeding Cash—and then found myself reading it again.

"Barry," I told him the next day, "you've really got something here. It's easy to read and it can be a series of publications, especially with so many changes constantly happening in today's financial world—and with everyone seemingly trying to get your cash."

I quickly realized that Barry already knew this.

Stop Bleeding Cash is an important book for everyone to read, whether young or old, regardless of financial status or stage of life. It's truly amazing how much cash just slips through our hands or jumps out of our pockets and wallets when there is another, often better solution.

Barry Waxler's book, Stop Bleeding Cash, will remind you of cash-draining and money-stealing traits and traps that we've all experienced and forgotten about. After you read it, you're going to think twice before reaching into your pocket, and you'll realize in a short period of time that many overpriced "deals" are scams and schemes created solely to drain you of your cash—and that they can be avoided.

Stop Bleeding Cash is one of those books you're going to want to keep handy as a reference work at home and at the office, and have family read—even young children in your household. And you'll definitely want to recommend it to your friends and associates.

It's fascinating how spending a windy day on a sailboat in San Diego's big bay, with a crew member you've met for the first time, can result in a long-lasting personal and professional relationship, one that you're willing to share with everyone you know.

Oh, how did we do in that sailboat race in 1992? We were first in our division—and I'm confident that you too will find reading Stop Bleeding Cash a winning experience.

Urban Miyares
President, Disabled Businesspersons Association

Preface

The Great Give Back

When I started my career back in the mid 1980s, the goal was to find as many people as I could to help as much as I could. There was a whirlwind of activities, and I found that my intentions were good, but my direction was off. The net result was that everything I did was predicated on current legislation, and I found myself having to reinvent myself every two years. Is that really how we want to spend our careers? When I tried to help people out, it was always a one-at-a-time project, and many times we had to circle the wagons and undo the effects of the plan because of changing legislation.

Since the effects of 9/11 hit, we have seen many changing markets, and our country has fallen from the great power that it was and become a nation trying to find its direction. Automakers have gone by the wayside, banks that we knew and respected are gone, the mortgage and credit industry has been turned upside down, and the stock market has a higher level of volatility. Most important, consumer confidence has never fully recovered from this debacle, further separating the haves from the have nots.

I've found—and this has helped greatly in our circles—that if you want great gains, you have to step back and give back first. In other words, put your efforts where they make the greatest impact, which is not always in your own house.

In 2013, as I was writing this book, I was contacted by a renowned radio producer who has a history of producing great radio shows that we all know quite well. He said that I should be on radio now that I have a book that can be used to spread good information. Based on the compliance model of my industry, I took that into consideration, and at first I was very excited. Once the dust settled, however, my enthusiasm came back to earth. It dawned on me that if people really wanted to listen to me talk about Stop Bleeding Cash every week, my office would already have been flooded with more clients than I could talk to.

Just as I was ready to close the book on the radio platform, a friend of mine asked me to speak with a lady by the name of Andrea Kaye. By sheer coincidence, Andrea was on the same radio station that I had previously been considering. As a courtesy to my friend, I said I would sit down with her, even though I was 99 percent out of the game.

That was a day that changed my life—for good!

Andrea explained that her goal for the radio show was to use it to meet many of the great business people in our community, and by using the radio as leverage, to connect small-business owners and thereby enable them to work together and to network for the greater good of all. And the grand beneficiaries of this process would be those who read this book and listened to the new radio show.

And so, on September 26, 2013, Close Up On San Diego Business was born. On that day, we created a radio platform that interviews small business owners, teaching the listeners the unique facets of their businesses. We interview primarily home-grown businesses that are working to make a difference in our community. We have a renowned tax advisor as an alternating co-host, with a representative from one of the great nonprofit companies in town, and we always bring the local personality on air by inviting Andrea as our co-producer and co-host.

The way this plays out is that we no longer have to use the radio platform as a tool to find sponsors because we continually promote all the small businesses that work with us to make a better community. We network with these business owners to keep small business as a meaningful part of our community, and we focus resources to help grow the philanthropic values in our community.

We plan to grow this in other communities as time allows, by leveraging social media channels. By taking the show on location, we can generate more awareness of our cause. One of our goals is to take this to local high schools and show the students the value of giving back. Our society needs to take a step back and learn the value of giving back first.

Our community starts with small business. Close Up on San Diego Business focuses on helping small businesses stay strong. I tell every guest on my show, every week, that if the Walmarts and Costcos of the world wanted to be in our business, we wouldn't be there! The appreciation level for what we do is so wonderful, and to be candid, it gives me a sense of accomplishment unlike any I have experienced.

When I worked for a small-business owner back in the early 1980s, they always taught me the value of synergy, the idea that two great minds working in harmony can accomplish far more than each of us can accomplish by working separately.

If we are to succeed in business, as we wish to in life, rebuilding America starts here, with us. I have stated for years that my life and my career have been built by default, not by design. A harsh statement coming from a planner, but it is what it is.

Let's all get close up and see what we can do together.

INTRODUCTION
Stop Bleeding Cash!
Understanding How Money Works

Are you working so hard for your money that you don't have time to figure out what to do with it? If so, you're not alone. That's how it is for many people. They have a vague sense that they're bleeding cash.

And the problem is that they're right.

Taxes. Home loans. Credit card debt. Healthcare expenses. Business expenses. Insurance premiums. These are the six most common bleeding points. In each of these areas, things are set up to favor the government, the lender, or the service provider. The deck is stacked in their favor, not yours.

You work so hard for the money you earn. Wouldn't it be great to know exactly what to do to stop the bleeding? To shift the situation so that you come out ahead, not the IRS, the insurance company, or the bank?

Over the course of this book, I hope to show you how to stop the bleeding. I hope you will say what so many of my new clients have said over the years: "Why didn't I know that?" It's not that your intentions aren't good or that the people you have worked with in the past aren't trustworthy or capable. I just want to show you how to think outside the box and find the hidden solutions. That's what this book is all about.

Many people, even those who have a lot of cash, don't have a clue how money works. Because they don't know how money works, they are not able to plan properly. And many people, because they fail to plan properly, end up bleeding cash.

In this book we will show you where you may be losing money and how to stop the bleeding. It all starts with understanding how money works. If you understand how money works, you can do what you need to do in advance to plan and maximize your spendability. While everyone's situation is different and needs to be looked at independently, many people don't realize that the most important thing about money is not how much you earn, nor the rate of return, nor the return of your capital. It's all about what the maximum spendability of your money is.

What is spendability? Spendability (a phrase I coined based on my experience) is the difference between someone who makes a dollar and is able to spend fifty cents of that dollar, and somebody who makes a dollar and is able to spend seventy-five cents of that dollar. It's not how much you make; it's how much you can spend. How much of your hard-earned money can you actually spend? How much do you actually keep?

We want to make sure that you know how to keep the maximum amount of your money, to retain maximum spendability. If you are giving all your money away to taxes, to your home loan, to your credit card debt, to healthcare-related expenses, to business expenses, and to insurance premiums, then you are not maximizing your spendability.

The fact is, you can keep and spend much more of the money you make simply through creative planning. The problem many upper middle class people face is that they are so busy earning money, they don't have the time to take care of it properly. Think of the height of the real estate market—around 2004–2007, before the market crashed. You could buy a property for nothing down, and watch it go up 25 percent a year. Who was making money hand over fist during this period? Realtors.

Now, real estate agents generally work 24/7. When they're not hunting down listings, they're showing the sellers' properties. With their work schedule, these realtors couldn't possibly find the time to plan how to care for their money. They would walk into their accountant's office on April 14th and say, "Here's all my information; what do you want me to do?"

"Well," the accountant might say, "let's take out $40,000 and put it into a retirement plan through your 401(k)." And that would be it. It would be too late to do anything else. The realtor would be far too busy making money to save money, to plan to maximize their income.

In today's world, there are professions that are just like the realtors of the housing boom. Everyone is working 24/7. If you're successful, you have no time, because you're using all your time to work, or plan for work, or to think about how to get work done. It's the way of the world today: we don't have time.

This is a problem affluent people are often able to avoid. They have advisors who guide the growth, protection, and investment of their money. People in the upper middle class, on the other hand, may not be able to afford the advisors to do it for them. In my opinion, the advisors who work with the middle class like to keep things simple. This is good for the advisor, as the advisor doesn't have to learn all that much. It's also good for the company that generates the product they sell. However, it is often a disadvantage to the client. You are taking on all the risk, while the advisor and the issuer are protected. Nobody is looking out for you.

I believe that people are just biased toward simple. If anything is complex, they throw their hands up because it takes too much time to figure out and it's too hard to explain. But the truth is, the world isn't always simple. Sometimes you need a little bit of complication, otherwise you may end up buying a product that benefits the company more than it benefits you.

In my practice, we find opportunities by using tools that other advisors in the market don't even know about. Many advisors, like their upper middle-class clients, are working so hard earning money they don't have time to grasp these new concepts. Moreover, these solutions usually don't bring the advisor any money up front, so why would they bother with them?

In my practice, we look out for you. We find hidden opportunities that you didn't know were available to you. Every toolbox has unused tools; we want to help you find those tools and use them. We put all the solutions on the table, whether we make money from them or not.

I can show you how you can leverage your bank relationship by employing an investment and a checking account, or by utilizing your retirement plan to pay off your other debt. I've always taken what appears to be very simple, made it very complicated, and then broken it back down into simple pieces to attack it. I am very thorough in what I do because one size does not fit all. Clients trust me because I lay out a laundry list of what is going on with each individual client. I work hard to create a relationship of trust with my clients. I find things that other people may miss, because I do discovery work.

I have twenty-eight years of experience in the investment services industry, but before that, I have always been a creative thinker and problem solver. I graduated high school thanks to my ingenuity. I didn't have great grades or attendance, but I knew how to do things in a creative way in order to get by. When I got into the financial planning business, I found that I loved working with people. I loved creating solutions. I loved helping people with things they didn't know how to do.

About ten or twelve years ago, I went with one of my colleagues to visit an accountant who had just moved into a new office. We sat down in her conference room, and we all noticed something strange about the wall. It was a stucco wall with glass blocks. All of the glass blocks were in perfect order, all grouped together…except for one, which was sitting all by itself. My colleague looked over at the accountant and asked, "Why is the wall like that?"

"I don't know," the accountant said. "I just moved in here. I've been trying to figure it out myself."

I looked over at both of them. "I understand it," I said. "That's the way I live my life."

The two of them looked at me funny. "What do you mean?" they asked. "What are you talking about?"

"That," I said, "is living outside the box."

I live outside the box because I love to do creative things. Some people are creative because they can do wonderful things with their hands, like building or remodeling houses. The last thing you ever want to see is me with a screwdriver in my hand! But I love the creative side of finance. I love finding solutions.

And this book can help you to find yours.

Chapter 1
Are You Bleeding Cash?

Let's start with a classic example of a little-known solution: two products that do basically the same thing, but in a very different way.

Please note that the following example provides an over-simplified scenario that may or may not be appropriate for your financial situation. Each product, service, or approach referenced serves a specific purpose with features, risks, and expenses that need to be considered in relation to each client's needs and objectives.

The first product is a fixed annuity. Depending on your situation, you may buy an annuity in your name because you don't have to pay taxes on the annuity earnings today. So you buy an annuity and put $100,000 into it. For the sake of illustration, the $100,000 grows to a million dollars because you don't make any withdrawals or spend any of the money. But when that lump sum comes out of the annuity, a considerable portion of it may be taxable. Annuities provide income that is taxable as ordinary income in the taxpayer's current income tax bracket. In our example, the annuity is a non-qualified annuity, or one that is personally owned and not included in the owner's retirement plan. In this case, any earnings apply to taxes and any principal returned is not taxed according to current tax laws.

If you understand the various products available, including their unique features and expenses, you could consider a life insurance product instead of an annuity. You'll get the same tax deferral, but because of the way you buy it, you may increase your rate of return with no additional market risk. Why? Because in my opinion a fixed annuity is considered a short-term product by the insurance company, whereas a life insurance policy is considered a long-term product. (Annuities are considered long-term investments designed for retirement purposes. Withdrawals of taxable amounts are subject to income tax, and if taken prior to age 59½, a 10% federal tax penalty may apply. Early withdrawals may be subject to withdrawal charges. Optional riders have limitations and are available for an additional cost through the purchase of a variable annuity contract. Guarantees are based on the claims-paying ability of the issuing company.)

By doing this, you can go from the lower earnings capacity of a short-term product, such as a fixed annuity, to the higher earnings capacity of a long-term product such as a life insurance product. Typically, the returns in an indexed annuity have earned less than an insurance product designed in a similar fashion. The annuity has a lower maximum earning rate because of the institution's ability to buy the index option in a short-term environment, which is governed by your local department of insurance, while the life insurance product is designed as a long term vehicle, allowing a different type of indexed option purchase. This follows the guidelines of short-term interest rates, and as such has produced annuity caps on earnings in the current environment of about 4 percent while the life insurance product's long term investment earnings may allow caps on earnings in the range of 10 percent or more in some instances. While life insurance has an inherent cost of insurance, our experience tells us that the net earnings on investment of the life insurance product will exceed the annuity in many positive markets, and be similar to the annuity in most down markets. (Short-term products referenced are considered annuities, and as such, carriers producing them must set aside reserves in accordance with products that are to be liquid for income in nature. The net result of this is that the options purchased for interest returns are more expensive, and returns are expected to be less. Long-term products such as life insurance policies have less stringent reserve guidelines and offer carriers the ability to purchase more competitive index options. Long-term options can offer potential rates of return equaling twice or more of that offered by short term products in an identical market.) You'll get the same tax deferral, but you'll get more liquidity—sometimes as much as 90 percent liquidity on a life insurance product versus 10 percent on the typical annuity product.

The costs of life insurance and annuities differ greatly. Annuities rarely have a death benefit in excess of the current accumulation or earning value. Life insurance policies typically have a mortality cost associated with them, making them a much more expensive product on the surface. On the flip side, however, annuities have a lower earning capacity, since the insurance company can use only short-term investment options to buy its inherent rate of return. Life insurance products are considered long-term investments, and by insurance code they have a higher potential yield by virtue of the long-term option pricing the insurance industry has within its portfolios. If you look at life insurance, your primary consideration is whether you need the death benefit, and as such, are willing to cover the cost of the insurance inside the policy. Comparing the two products in identical market conditions, and by product guidelines as dictated by the issuing carrier, should usually show the net effect in most circumstances.

The biggest difference is that with an annuity, when you die, your heir will have to pay taxes on $900,000 of that million-dollar annuity example. However, if you have a million-dollar life insurance product, it converts into an income-tax-free death benefit. You just saved your heirs all of the income taxes on $900,000 worth of earnings.

We work to find overlooked opportunities in your business or personal finance arena. We find the money you are throwing away somewhere else. It may be in your hard costs, such as mortgages or insurance products. It may be in soft costs, such as taxes. If I can, for example, reduce your tax load, you'll end up with money that you can put away for your future.

In truth, taxes are the number-one place where people bleed cash unnecessarily. Much of the planning for keeping your money is centered on taxes. If I sit in the affluent category, I don't typically hire an accountant to do my taxes. I hire a tax strategist, because I need advanced tax strategy to manage my money and minimize my taxes.

If I am an upper middle class guy, making two or three hundred thousand bucks a year, then I hire an accountant to take all the historical figures and plug them into the tax return. That doesn't involve a lot of strategizing. I consider the average accountant to be a historian. When you walk into the accountant's office with your shoebox full of receipts, the accountant will tally them up and put them into a line.

Every once in a while you run into an accountant who is a strategist, who looks for solutions to help the bottom line. However, many accountants don't strategize, usually because they simply don't have the time. Many accountants do the vast majority of their work in in a small window of time, since the majority of people crunch their taxes in right before the deadline. How would an accountant have time in that crunch to strategize new solutions? All they can do is ask the basic questions they're used to asking.

People have accountants who simply say, "Brace yourself; this is what you owe." Those accountants are historians, just putting in the historical data. If you want them to do tax strategizing you'll have to ask. Asking an accountant to do tax strategizing is always a matter of timing. If you go to your accountant in November or December, he or she will probably have time to talk to you. But if you go between January and April, or even from May to September, he or she is most likely going to have other clients waiting on the line or sitting in their office.

How can your accountant have time to stop and think about your stuff? When you arrive, he'll say, "Okay, here's your shoebox. We're going to put this receipt in this line and that receipt in that line." You can't get individual attention unless you press your accountant when he or she has dead time—and in my opinion, few accountants have enough dead time even in November or December to stop and focus on a specific client.

So what do you do if you don't have the $500 an hour to hire a tax strategist? How do you create strategies? In my practice, we create the strategies that the accountants—the historians—can consider for your filings. We put your assets in a position for potential growth. We provide the tools to show you how to build and protect your assets.

We attempt to work with you to think ahead, strategize, and package it up so the historians know where to put it. In this way, we can complement the work accountants do. We're not looking to take our clients to different accountants. We look to work within the advisory circles in which the client is already working. We will assist with your planning earlier in the tax reporting year. Then you can take those solutions to your tax professional. If we can create benefits that the accountant agrees with, we both win. The accountant can even take that benefit to someone else.

This is something people don't realize: although income taxes are mandatory, estate taxes are voluntary. You don't have to pay a dime of estate taxes if you don't want to. All you have to do is plan to minimize estate taxes for your heirs. It is possible to work toward the lowest possible level of income taxes, but we can't eliminate them. However, we can work to eliminate or minimize estate taxes. Just by gifting out your entire estate while you live, you can avoid estate taxes—and that is far from the only or best way to do it!

Although probably the most prevalent, taxes are only one place in which the upper middle class suffers needlessly. Everybody has expenses they incur on a regular basis. What we do is find more ways to diminish those expenses, or make them tax-deductible. Our goal is to improve your bottom line.

We will assist you in reviewing out-of-pocket care-related expenses—medical, dental, vision care, and child care—for in order to determine whether they are tax-deductible. In many cases, those figures alone can add up a considerable portion of your income.

Please note that the following example provides an over-simplified scenario that may or may not be appropriate for your financial situation. Each product, service, or approach referenced serves a specific purpose with features, risks, and expenses that need to be considered in relation to each client's needs and objectives.

Perhaps you have a home loan weighing you down. When the housing market recently crashed, much of the equity went with it; and when the equity was gone, so was the credit. Many people today may not be able to refinance their home loans because they don't have sufficient equity. They may modify their loans, but many people are just sitting with six and seven percent loans, and they can't do a thing with them. They can't get their money out. We can provide references to other professionals who may be able to provide loan modifications, depending on the unique facts and circumstances of each particular client and property.

Please note that the following example provides an over-simplified scenario that may or may not be appropriate for your financial situation. Each product, service, or approach referenced serves a specific purpose with features, risks, and expenses that need to be considered in relation to each client's needs and objectives.

You could also have credit-card debt draining your cash away. So many people are paying double-digit interest on their credit cards, when we are in a 0–1% interest market. Instead of continuing to pay that exorbitant rate, you can take that double-digit interest, convert it to single-digit interest, and make yourself the bank to pay that interest off. How? By going into your 401(k) plan and borrowing enough money to pay off your credit cards, and then repaying the 401(k) for the loan. All of a sudden, you'll go from a potential of 10–15% interest down to a more reasonable potential of 2–3% interest—and you'll be paying that interest to yourself. Everyone's situation is different, and this is just one possible example, understanding that an unexpected job loss or job opportunity with a new employer would make the entire 401(k) loan immediately due and payable. This risk may outweigh the benefit in a climate of employment uncertainty or when career or employment changes are possible. This type of action would also require increased personal commitment to refrain from accumulating additional credit card debt until the 401(k) loan has been repaid in full, along with full understanding that there will be lost investment opportunity in the 401(k) due to the withdrawal and realization that the loan will be repaid with after-tax dollars rather than before-tax dollars.

These are just a few examples of how you can save yourself from bleeding cash in these common areas. It all comes back to understanding how money works. There are many more facets to understanding money. You have to understand how the location of your money affects things. Say you have college-age kids, and you have $250,000 sitting in your bank account or sitting in a mutual fund account. You're getting ready to use that $250,000 for college. Is that money going to help you or hurt you when you apply for college loans, college grants, and college financial aid?

Please note that the following example provides an over-simplified scenario that may or may not be appropriate for your financial situation. Each product, service, or approach referenced serves a specific purpose with features, risks, and expenses that need to be considered in relation to each client's needs and objectives.

In college planning, if you have money in a bank account or a mutual fund, it seems to count against you when applying for financial aid. However, if you take that money and put it into a life insurance policy or an annuity, it may not count against you. You could have $100–$150,000 invested in mutual funds and not qualify for financial aid. But you could have money sitting in protected products—e.g., retirement plans, real estate, annuities, and life insurance—and you may qualify for some amount of financial aid assistance for your student. It appears to be in your positioning. Part of planning involves deciding where to keep your money in consideration of both your short- and long-term financial circumstances. Moving investments into different types of products may or may not appropriate for your specific situation, as the unique risks, features, and expenses of each product need to be carefully considered in relation to the short-term benefit that it may provide.

The truth is, time is the single greatest asset you own. Time is everything, and timing is everything. If my money doubles on December 31st, I'm going to be seriously tax challenged. But if I know my money is going to double on December 31st, I can do something to plan for that on December 15th. We can use time to our advantage.

Timing is exactly why I am writing this book now. Although the information in this book may be timeless, and will always be important and valid, it is especially timely now. Tax laws can change, and it is always wise to stay on top of changing legislation.

If you had the choice, would you want to pay taxes in a low-tax environment or a high-tax environment? Naturally, you'd want to pay in a low-tax environment. Meanwhile, you are probably putting money away into a qualified retirement plan. Here's the catch: you are putting money away while you are in a low-tax environment. When you take it out, you should consider the possibility of being in a high-tax environment.

"But when I retire," many people protest, "I'm going to be in a lower tax bracket." In my opinion, there's only one reason why you would be in a lower tax bracket when you retire: because you failed along the way. If you succeed along the way, and if you have a plan for retirement, then you're going to have as much income when you retire as when you were working. Say you put away $100,000 when you are in a 28% tax bracket, and the money grows to a million dollars by the time you retire. By that time, tax rates will most likely have gone up—they have to. When you begin taking money out, you could potentially be in a 45% tax bracket.

Why do we practice this counterproductive saving? In my opinion, it is because the government beats it into our heads. Remember that the U.S. government is one of the largest banks on the face of the earth. The government promotes the practice of saving all the money you can in a tax-free environment, because it is basically a savings account for the government. You may be able to put $100,000 away, get a double-digit rate of return, and have a million dollars when you retire—and so does the government. They are your partner, but you are the one taking all the risk. Whether you like them or not, whether you want them or not, we all have partners out there. The government is our partner in many things.

In my practice, we are committed to finding those win-win situations that will help you understand how money works and stop you from bleeding cash...and those solutions are exactly what we want to introduce you to in this book.

Please note that the following examples provide an over-simplified scenario that may or may not be appropriate for your financial situation. Each product, service, or approach referenced serves a specific purpose with features, risks, and expenses that need to be considered in relation to each client's needs and objectives.

If you could predict the day your retirement account would suffer its greatest loss, you would be able to prepare for that day. In my opinion, the day your retirement account will suffer its greatest loss is the day you pay taxes on it. This may happen every time you make a withdrawal in retirement.

If you could find a way to achieve only earnings and block out losses for your heirs after your death, you could prepare to protect your principal. This goes back to annuity versus life insurance policy. When an insurance company buys options, they basically take your money and stick it into a long-term bond portfolio. They know the money is going to sit there and earn about 5% over the long haul.

Since it is going to be earning 5%, they give you two choices: you can stick your money in there and earn 3–4% while they carry a 1% spread with no market risk; or you can buy an option, which means that out of the 5% earnings on your money, they're going to take that 3–4% they would normally pay you and use it to buy an option against one of the indexes. If that option comes in, you will get the returns that are inside that option. Depending on the claim-paying ability of the issuer, you could achieve earnings on your principal.

If you could increase your liquidity without sacrificing anything, you could also prepare for that. You can increase your liquidity depending on the type of product you are in. There are a variety of available products that can be considered in light of your financial circumstances, objectives, time horizon, and risk tolerance.

If you could ensure that your heirs could have access to all of your money, and bypass the death tax, wouldn't you? Again, planning is everything. Let's say you have five or six or eight million dollars worth of assets. You buy a three-million-dollar life insurance policy because you want to make sure you have liquidity for your heirs. If that life insurance policy is held in your name or in a family trust, the money applies to your estate. You might circumvent the income tax on it, but the death tax will still kick in and take half your money, even in a life insurance policy.

However, by working with legal counsel, we may identify a way to get that life insurance policy owned outside your estate so that the money that goes to your heirs becomes tax free. It just requires identifying the right estate plan ahead of time. If you own the money that you're trying to pass on to your children, it could work against you. If you set it up in a simple trust where you still control it, but you don't own it, then it doesn't work against you.

Finally, if you could learn how to implement this, you would want to, wouldn't you? In this book, we will introduce you to these concepts and help you understand how you can stop bleeding cash!

CHAPTER TWO
How to Stop the Bleeding
on Your Taxes

The actions of the government, in the form of taxes, will have a bigger impact on your money than almost anything else. And the truth is, income taxes and estate taxes are only two of the dozens of taxes that may affect your future. Just in your day to day life, you face social security taxes, property taxes, school taxes, energy taxes, telephone taxes, capital gains taxes—the list goes on and on. Basically, the only things that aren't taxed are those that are illegal.

The sheer amount you pay in taxes every year is staggering. Fortunately, there are ways to avoid paying unnecessary taxes, and to avoid more taxes than you need to—ways that go far beyond merely using a qualified plan.

Early in my career, I ran across a letter from United States Supreme Court Justice Louis Brandeis that made a huge impact on my life. The letter read:

"I live in Alexandria, Virginia. Near the Supreme Court chambers is a toll bridge across the Potomac. When in a rush, I pay the dollar toll and get home early. However, I usually drive outside the downtown section of the city and across the Potomac on a free bridge.

If I went over the toll bridge and through the barrier without paying the toll, I would be committing tax evasion.

If, however, I drive the extra mile and drive outside the city of Washington to the free bridge, I am using a legitimate, logical, and suitable method of tax avoidance, and I am performing a useful social service by doing so. For my tax evasion, I should be punished. For my tax avoidance, I should be commended. The tragedy of life today is that so few people know the free bridge even exists."

Finding the free bridge is more important today than ever. As I remember it, back in the late 1970s and early 1980s, when Jimmy Carter was in office, tax rates were ridiculously high. If you had an income of roughly $400,000, you would pay a 70% tax on anything over that $400,000. Then, on top of that 70% tax, you would have estate taxes. You could literally walk away with zero dollars. Your kids could literally walk away with zero dollars. Some people were paying up to 90–95% taxes. In my eyes, that's bordering on communism. On top of all this, interest rates were in the double digits.

In my opinion, this was one of the ugliest times in American history. Home values were in decline, and it was not until Carter left office that things started to look up. When Ronald Reagan came into office, he began to focus on spurring business growth. He started to bring tax rates down, and people were once again able to afford to be in business.

Since the Carter administration, tax rates have plummeted to an all-time low. We are now in the lowest marginal tax rate we are likely to experience anytime in the foreseeable future. Unfortunately, the federal government's only source of revenue is taxes, and the problem is that the government spends more than it collects. The Obama administration has quadrupled the American deficit, and the only way we can pay it down is higher tax rates. The federal debt is growing exponentially, and the labor force in this country is declining, and will continue to do so. Meanwhile, the number of retirees who subsist on government programs such as Social Security and Medicare is on the rise, and those retirees are living longer and longer. There will soon be fewer taxpaying workers than ever. If the government raises interest rates substantially, they will destroy the real estate market, and with it, the American Dream. In my opinion, the only answer is increasing the tax rates.

While the current administration has said that they are only going to go after the income levels above $250,000, they have raised the estate (death tax) exemption to $5,430,000 per person ($10,860,000 per marriage). This means that fewer estates are in the estate-tax-paying bracket, and the bigger planning needs now lie in income tax planning. And while the burden is now on the income tax planning, I believe that it is only a matter of time before they go right back and attack the estate. It is all very confusing.

For me, this rising tax environment is a key area of concern. I think that the government knows how money works, and they hide the truth from the general public. If you listen to your parents, you will expect to be in a lower tax bracket when you retire. That is outdated thinking from the 1940s and 1950s, when every company built a retirement plan for its employees. The average employee lived to be sixty-two years old, and the company could use your money to retire your neighbors. This worked well for companies until the entire country started living longer. Now the fastest growing segment of America is the centenarians, the people who live to be 100. All the post-war era money is gone.

If you achieve your financial goals for retirement, you will have at least as much income as when you were working, if not more. If we have increasing tax rates, you could be biting your nose off to spite your face.

Why? Well, let's assume that you are paying an average tax rate now, say 28 percent. If you succeed in your financial goals, you should have just as much money when you retire as you do today. This means that when you retire, you will be in the same income range as you are today. Now imagine that the tax rates rise, as is almost inevitable, and the marginal tax rate hits a hypothetical 45% maximum bracket, and you fall into that. Say you were incredibly fortunate and you earned enough to double the money in your retirement plan. You now have twice as much money as when you started. You put your money away in a 28% bracket, so you have saved 28% in taxes on half of it. But when you pull it out in retirement, you will be paying 45% on the whole thing. Why would you want to save money from taxes in the lowest tax bracket you have ever seen, just to grow that money tax deferred and take it out in a higher bracket?

I once heard a wise man say, "Rich people think like rich people, and poor people think like poor people." It is my belief that the biggest difference between the two is that rich people know how money works, and can figure out how to make the adjustments to save taxes, leaving the heaviest tax burden to the masses.

Mandy and Gabe came to me just in advance of Gabe's retirement date. Their concern was the effects of an increasing tax environment in retirement. Gabe had worked forty years as a successful engineer in the aerospace industry. He did not want to see all of his hard earned income and assets go to the government with a new administration on a spending spree. They had about $1,000,000 in retirement funds and about $7,000,000 in assets, including a substantial real estate portfolio. Gabe's goal was to use the declining real estate market to leverage his retirement income, even though his employer took care of most of his income needs, at least in the beginning of the retirement phase.

At the conclusion of our analysis and after our work with tax and legal counsel, $200,000 was re-characterized from taxable income to tax-free profits in the combined Roth IRAs for Mandy and Gabe. Another $30,000 was converted to a tax-deductible format using the other plans within the plan, including a fully funded program to put their four grandchildren through college in the years to come. This is just an example of the results that can be achieved with a successful plan. Your results may vary, simply because every situation is unique.

Another integrated tax plan involved Rick and Stella, who sold their business for $21,000,000; their share was $6,000,000 after all expenses. They had the choice of paying the tax (some ordinary income and the balance capital gains), or again, getting creative with their integrated tax plan. In this case, we needed to bring in highly advanced tax counsel. The plan involved setting up some business entities for their continued business needs, and applying a marketing and management style planning method. By doing that, we were able not only to defer the tax payment due date, but also to add more retirement plan contributions and a charitable lead annuity trust, and to build tax savings. Now they are able to make contributions over the next fifteen years to their charities of choice, have that money invested for the long term, and any excess not contributed to charities by the trust guidelines returns to their family at the end of the fifteen years, including any investment returns during that period. This is just another example of the results of a successful plan. Again, your results may vary because every situation is unique.

There are solutions to the problem of rising tax rates. I think that we are all brainwashed into thinking we need to use government savings plans in order to survive. These plans are marketed by everyone from banks to brokers. But more often than not, if you look closely, the tax savings and deferral programs sponsored by the government end up helping the government and the companies far more than they help the taxpayer. So if putting money into a retirement account isn't the solution, what are the other options for saving money on taxes? There are myriad possible ways to use your retirement plan to pay for things with pre-tax dollars that you would normally pay for with after-tax dollars.

First and foremost, take as much of your income used for non-deductible expenses as you can and find a way to make them deductible. The self-employed world has been doing this for years. You may be able to make all of your out-of-pocket medical, dental, vision care, and child care expenses pre-tax. You may be able to pay your life insurance premiums from a tax-deductible source. You may be able to move your credit card debt to a source that can be deductible. The list goes on.

You just need to find a way to get the government to participate in your plan. Most people simply want a hard cost reduction. The affluent, however, know how to make traditionally non-deductible costs deductible. Learn how money works for the institutions and government, and you will see how you can make them your allies, and possibly take all those savings and put them into your future. Use retirement plan rules to your advantage, and maximize Roth programs for maximum tax-free growth. If you are investing in real estate and the program is strong enough, you can even take a Roth IRA with little money in it and convert it to a self-directed program that could leverage your tax-free savings into a retirement opportunity.

Does the government pay you a substantial tax refund every

year? You may want to consider that an interest-free loan to the government every year. In fact, the only reason you get a refund is because you overpaid during the year. Then you ask for your money back when you file the tax return. Does the government pay you interest on that money you loan them? No. They don't even thank you for using your money while they had it.

Why do we have to work so hard to get our tax refunds at the end of the year, when in reality that money should have been ours all along? Think about the size of your tax refund. For an average income, that refund is probably a couple of thousand dollars at least. Now imagine how useful that money would have been if you could have used it over the course of the year! Many people could use that money to pay the high interest rates on their credit cards, instead of allowing it to accumulate while the government uses your money.

What we want to do is maximize what you do during the year in order to minimize the amount you are overpaying the government. That way you get to use that money during the year, instead of the government using it free of charge. Take control of your money and your future, or they will. Learn the ins and outs of how money works, and you will make government and institutions your allies.

Banks will loan directly to your retirement plan on a non-recourse basis. Let the risk lie with the government, not your personal assets. As a matter of fact, one of the key things we teach while building great wealth is to protect the wealth you have now, as well as the wealth you are targeting for your portfolio. It is a well-known fact that government makes the rules that you are told to follow. I believe that when you learn how money really works, you can learn how to use government rules and government money for your retirement, instead of contributing to excessive government spending, as many people are doing right now.

It has been said that saving money won't make you rich, but leveraging the money you have will. Take the risk off of your back, and stop bleeding cash on your taxes!

CHAPTER THREE
How to Stop the Bleeding on Your Home Loan

In the early 2000s, the mortgage market was going like gang-busters. Around this time, a key phrase came into existence: mortgage planning. When mortgages were easy and plentiful, there were creative professionals who wanted an advantage and created a professional designation called mortgage planning.But their creativity ran out as soon as the easy loans became difficult.

A mortgage planner would take someone who wanted more home than they could afford and put the borrower into loans that had low payments—sometimes artificially low payments. Sometimes they would put the borrower into an Option ARM (Adjustable Rate Mortgage) loan, which was a loan that allowed a borrower to make any one of three payment options each month:

Principal and Interest

Interest Only

Negative Amortization (paying less than the interest charges each month, simultaneously driving your principal balance up)

In my opinion, these Option ARM loans were easy to sell, but not healthy for the banks. Ultimately, the banks suffered and needed a government bailout. However, the so-called "mortgage planners" did not even tell the clients who didn't lose their homes how to recapture the interest they had deferred and use it as a deductible item in the present day. In some cases, the clients lost $50,000 to $100,000 or more in tax deductions.

What many people didn't realize, and what I had to teach in my seminars, was that any time you defer interest on a loan and refinance it, that deferred interest is repaid. However, sometimes, if you didn't point it out to your tax advisor, the advisor would assume it was the principal pay down, when in fact it was deferred interest payback. By avoiding that mistake and asking questions, we were able to assist people in identifying considerable tax deductions on their tax returns because they had previously paid deferred interest when they refinanced.

Since the crash, the environment has become substantially different than it was in the early 2000s. Utilizing home equity is a thing of the past. Without it, we cannot refinance our homes. Therefore, people may be paying 6 to 7% in today's 3 to 4% environment. Many so-called mortgage planners are out of the business, and virtually all of the mortgage banks built out of that era are bankrupt and gone. For the most part, only the portfolio lenders are left.

I have many clients who come to me looking for assistance in obtaining relief from these high interest rates. It is simple to determine where the best results lie. The government has issued programs for public relief to circumvent the foreclosure market. Many people today try calling the banks and doing their own loan modifications. While that was sometimes possible in the early days of the program, the market has changed.

Today, just as you need an attorney to go to court, you need a loan modification specialist to talk with the banks. Whether you are suing somebody for a million dollars or facing the criminal justice system, when you go to court, you have an attorney represent you. Why? Because they know the court, they know the language, and they know the system. In my opinion, the same is true in modifying a loan. The bank has a system for loan modifications that the general public doesn't understand. No matter the size of the loan, you need representation. If a bank knows you are represented by someone other than yourself, they will respect you that much more.

Loan modifications can help you immensely. They are substantially cheaper and more effective than a refinance. Granted, there are no guarantees that your modification will go through, but the same is essentially true for a refinance; you have a financial risk either way. Loan modifications have been exhausted in many areas, but there appears to always be some market for them in a hardship capacity.

Julia came to me in a total financial crunch. She was a divorced female who had just turned 65, and had been laid off by the school district in one of their cutbacks. While she did eventually find employment with a local law firm, her income and hours were dialed way back, leaving her with approximately two thirds the income to which she was accustomed. The only substantial area in which she could cut back was her mortgage.

Julia owned a condominium that had been worth $400,000 at its peak. Due to the economic decline, the value of this condo had fallen to about $250,000. Unfortunately the debt between a first and second trust deed was well over $300,000, closing in on $350,000.

Her first request was to refinance the property. I was forced to give her the bad news that real estate lenders only lend on equity, and since she had none, there was nothing she could do in terms of a refinance. It wasn't like the good old days of stated income, when all you needed was a heartbeat and a checkbook in order to find a lender.

Due to government programs that were set up for people exactly like Julia, a loan modification was in order.

Please note that the following example provides an over-simplified scenario that may or may not be appropriate for your financial
situation. Each product, service, or approach referenced serves a
specific purpose with features, risks, and expenses that need to
be considered in relation to each client's needs and objectives.

Along with loan modifications, one important thing to learn
about mortgage planning is how to find and use lines of credit
effectively. If you have a second mortgage on your home, the
lender may be very flexible in modifying that loan. In the event
of foreclosure, the second-trust deed lenders know that they are
unlikely to get much when you lose your home. This can be great
leverage to use when negotiating the loan modification. If you
do not have a second mortgage or line of credit on your home,
it may be a good thing to look into. Using your line of credit in
lieu of credit cards or other unsecured debt can be a helpful tool.

If you do have equity in your home, you can gain control of
and use that equity by establishing an equity line of credit, which
essentially establishes your own personal "bank." This can help
your personal finances in many ways. However, it might surprise
you to hear that having equity in your home is not the be all and
end all of saving money on home loans. In my opinion, paying
cash up front for a home actually doesn't save you the money
you think it does. If you pay cash, that money is gone; you can't
invest it. Moreover, you don't get the mortgage tax deduction
for the coming years. Each strategy depends on your unique
circumstances, objectives, time horizon, and risk tolerance.

Not only can paying cash up front cause you to bleed away
money, but having a shorter-term mortgage can also make you
lose cash. A thirty-year mortgage may actually save (and make!)

you more money than a fifteen-year mortgage. Additionally, putting down money on your mortgage won't save you more money, despite what the banks tell you. Say you put down $40,000 on your thirty-year mortgage. The bank has use of that money for the next thirty years, instead of you. Yes, your monthly payments would be smaller, but if you had kept that $40,000, it could be making you money instead. Moreover, that $40,000 wouldn't even be tax-deductible! You want to make sure whatever money you put down is accessible to you, which can be achieved through an equity line of credit. Each strategy depends on your unique circumstances, objectives, time horizon, and risk tolerance.

Banks and mortgage companies are in it for one reason only: to collect as much interest as they can. By thinking outside the box and utilizing loan modifications and lines of credit, you can become your own bank, keeping the fees and high interest rates for yourself and your family. You can keep more of your money, and stop bleeding cash on your home loan. These types of strategies require discipline and a strong credit score to be successful.

CHAPTER FOUR
How to Stop the Bleeding on Your Credit Card Debt

In my opinion, credit card companies have always been unscrupulous, but in recent years they have become extremely so. They tease you with reasonable interest rates to get your account, and as soon as the initial period ends, they start adjusting rates. They give you a due date for the payments, and a "grace period" after the due date to send your payment in.

If your payment comes in during the grace period, there is no penalty. However, they still hold it against you. As soon as you send a payment in past the due date they start adjusting the rates on the cards and driving the interest up. What starts out as anywhere from 0–7% quickly adjusts to 10–20%. And if you regularly pay "late," those rates can go substantially higher.

The problem I have observed is that many small-business owners use credit cards for their everyday business activities. When the rates get out of control, cash flow problems in their business multiply. Even though the credit market has been extremely tight since 2007, most business owners don't know how to deal with this problem.

Please note that the following example provides an over-simplified scenario that may or may not be appropriate for your financial situation. Each product, service, or approach referenced serves a specific purpose with features, risks, and expenses that need to be considered in relation to each client's needs and objectives.

In my opinion, the answer lies in finding a way to be your own bank, to pay yourself the fees that you would normally be paying to a banking institution. Say, for example, that a business owner is paying $500 a month for his credit card. Because he is paying the bank the minimum payment, the entire payment is interest. While that interest may be tax-deductible, it never pays down the card balance. If, however, the business owner uses an alternative account that includes retirement plan assets, he can save the exorbitant interest rates the bank charges, and pay himself back instead.

To take another example, let's say you have a $25,000 line of credit and $100,000 in a 401(k) plan. You want to pay the interest on your credit card, which has gone into double-digit interest rates—let's say 10%. At the same time, you have a fluctuating 401(k) plan, which isn't necessarily earning anything, although it may go up or down 10%.

Now, if you could, wouldn't you want to have a guaranteed rate of return on your 401(k), while simultaneously not having to pay the 10% interest on your credit card? You can do this simply by taking money out of your 401(k) via a 401(k) loan subject to the provisions of your 401k plan document, paying off your credit card, and making that monthly payment back to yourself. By doing this, you could save 10% interest on the credit card—which may or may not be deductible—and you are paying yourself back, with interest, at whatever rate you or your employer set. You are taking the money that would have gone to a bank and giving it back to yourself instead. For your ability to achieve this, please refer to your 401k plan administrator. Everyone's situation is different, and this is just one possible example, understanding that an unexpected job loss or job opportunity with a new employer would make the entire 401(k) loan immediately due and payable. This risk may outweigh the benefit in a climate of employment uncertainty or when career or employment changes are possible. This type of action would also require increased personal commitment to refrain from accumulating additional credit card debt until the 401(k) loan has been repaid in full, along with full understanding that there will be lost investment opportunity in the 401(k) due to the withdrawal and realization that the loan will be repaid with after tax dollars rather than before tax dollars.

Tactics such as these can be used not only for credit card debt, but for any unsecured debt you may have. I had one client who came to me with double-digit interest rates on two cars he had bought. He had messed up his credit and had outstanding medical bills, along with several other issues. We helped relieve his debt by manipulating his retirement plan. We took money from an IRA, put it back into his own 401(k), and paid off his cars, his credit cards, and his medical debt, and even helped him with an escrow he had just closed on a house simply by utilizing a 401(k) loan. The primary reason we were able to accomplish this was that this client was self employed, and therefore he was able to format the 401k plan document to his own specifications within the rules allowed by 401k plan legislation. The risks of this strategy may outweigh the benefit in a climate of business uncertainty. This type of action would also require increased personal commitment to refrain from accumulating additional credit card debt until the 401(k) loan has been repaid in full, along with full understanding that there will be lost investment opportunity in the 401(k) due to a withdrawal and realization that the loan will be repaid with after-tax dollars rather than before-tax dollars.

While there are many other alternatives for dealing with credit card and other unsecured debt, there is one thing certain: banks are in business for a profit. If you happen to be a Fortune 500 company or a multi-billion dollar private company, you can get the red carpet treatment. But if you are anyone else, they only take care of you when they have to.

You don't have to stand idly by. Use the tools you have to cut out the ridiculous credit card interest, and stop bleeding cash on your credit card debt.

CHAPTER FIVE
*Stop Bleeding Cash
on Your Healthcare Expenses*

Healthcare expenses include not only the direct cost of insurance, but the out-of-pocket costs not covered by the health insurance company as well. The way to reduce direct insurance costs is to do a full-scale comparison and breakout of the benefits and costs of available policies. Using an intense software product, you can hone in and find exactly what you want. Getting to the source of the benefit helps you define what you really want, and you can then find the lowest cost, since most companies build their products for their own benefit, in my opinion.

As we move into the full-fledged Obamacare era, it is critical first to understand the new laws and how they affect you, from the company and group planning down to benefits, costs, and penalties as assessed by the new laws. The likelihood of any company getting a true grasp of this from their independent broker is very low. The new laws have created a whole new job description in the health insurance field: that of a fee-based advisor who can break down and actually decrypt the laws.

In my experience, we are finding that people who do, in fact, hire these fee-based professionals can protect themselves against the egregious penalties and also gain access to software programs that can define the best program options. The net result of hiring one of these professionals can be a small fee and a considerable savings, sometimes being a substantial part of the plan costs. The sad part is that you will never know how much you will save until you actually pay the fee. However, in my opinion, it is a small, small price to pay to begin the proper planning steps.

Now, when it comes to out-of-pocket expenses, many people don't realize there are ways to reduce those costs as well. There are programs that drive all out-of-pocket costs for qualified expenses to a pre-tax expenditure by restructuring the costs to a premium for a supplemental health insurance program. If structured properly, not only do you avoid incurring any costs, but you also save up to 39 percent of the actual expenditures, in the form of taxes. (39.6% is the maximum tax rate at time of publication [2013]. Tax rates are subject to change, and your rates will be directly affected by your own tax return. Please consult your tax advisor for actual rates for your circumstance.) I have found that in some plans, you pay for your expenses twice, only to be reimbursed; what's more, you also risk losing the money you set aside to get the tax benefits. Properly structured, there is no extra expenditure, and you get the tax benefits immediately.

In my opinion, the two biggest components of the American Dream are home ownership and owning your own business. While we all understand the benefits and privileges of owning your home, the same is not true for self-employment ventures.

Please note that the following example provides an over-simplified scenario that may or may not be appropriate for your financial situation. Each product, service, or approach referenced serves a specific purpose with features, risks, and expenses that need to be considered in relation to each client's needs and objectives.

AAA Plumbing came to me during the heat of the workers' compensation insurance debacle in the early 2000s. Their issue arose from the fact that they were paying their employees top-dollar wages, including the cost of benefits, and their worker's compensation insurance cost was an additional 25–33 percent of the laborer's wage. This made it very difficult to cover the employees' needs and still stay in business. While nothing can legally eliminate that insurance cost, there was a way to negate it with substantial impact.

Here is a possible solution that could be considered with advice from tax counsel: By installing a supplemental health and welfare program sponsored by a qualified insurance company, any or all out-of-pocket expenses for the individual employee get deducted through payroll and reimbursed as an insurance claim. This must be installed at the company level and facilitated through the payroll department. Done correctly, it may function as a single payroll event, and the employee gets immediate recognition on the very same payroll. Income through payroll is taxable, but running the income through payroll reduction is non-taxable. Claims from the insurance company are also non-taxable.

There are several different avenues for reducing cost. You can increase your deductibles and find government-oriented programs to pay your out-of-pocket costs. There are health reimbursement accounts and health savings accounts. These accounts are set up by the government for different reasons, but they essentially allow you to try to increase your deductibility, and then set up side programs to put the money away to pay those out-of-pocket costs.

Regardless of what kind of health insurance product you have, you will always have an out-of-pocket, unreimbursed expense, whether it is medical, dental, or vision. If you have kids, you could easily spend a couple of thousand dollars a year in dental expenses. Any dental expense you incur is typically non-deductible, unless you are low income and qualify. The easiest way to make it deductible is to be self-employed and have no employees. However, very few people are in that position.

Typical group health products used by companies are set up so the employer pays a certain share and the employee pays a certain share. Let's say the employer pays 75 percent of the employee's healthcare insurance costs. That means 25 percent has to come out of the employee's pocket. If the employer pays none of the costs for the employee's dependents, the employee has to pay 100 percent of those costs out-of-pocket as well. For the average family, this could be $5000–$10,000 a year just in medical, dental, and vision care expenses.

Many companies will investigate using what is known as a "cafeteria plan" or "flexible spending account" under Section 125 of the Internal Revenue Code to cover out-of-pocket expenses. The cafeteria plan helps force you to put money away for unreimbursed medical, dental, vision, and child care expenses. Any unreimbursed expenses—meaning anything the insurance policy doesn't cover—are eligible for this plan.

The problem with a cafeteria plan is that it is a government program, which means it has government limits. You have to save the money, and you have to spend the money before the year is out. If you don't use all the money, it could just go back to the company and you will lose it. Therefore, in my opinion, most companies are very, very restrictive about setting up these programs.

To circumvent this problem for the self-employed or the small-business owner, it may be possible to locate a licensed insurance company that would set up an individual private program that produces similar results to the cafeteria (flexible spending) plan, and that may not subject clients to the same risks. There would be no "use it or lose it" rule, no having to save money before you spend it. On this type of plan, you can get the deduction after you incur the expense. (Rates and terms would be subject to change and unique to each carrier.)

The plan that I have seen applied is a fully insured supplemental group health insurance policy specifically designed to fill in gaps in primary health coverage. It takes any unreimbursed medical, dental, and vision expenses and runs them through payroll, covering up to $200,000 in expenses that would otherwise be paid with personal after-tax earnings.

The product typically works for any type of business structure—sole proprietorships, partnerships, LLCs and LLPs, Sub S and C corporations, and for-profit and not-for-profit corporations. The plan may cover everything from deductibles and co-payments to childbirth and pre/postnatal care, from health-related mileage, lodging, and meals to dental and vision care. It may also cover pre-existing conditions. Generally, if an expense is medically necessary and qualifies under Section 213 of the Internal Revenue Code, it may be eligible for reimbursement under the policy. It is important to review specific policy coverage and restrictions by carrier.

Plans typically offer a choice of annual maximums—either standard maximums of $50,000, $100,000, or $200,000, or custom benefit levels—and a per occurrence maximum equal to 10 percent of the annual maximum. As an example, an annual base premium of $250 covers either an employee or the employee and all eligible dependents. In many cases, there may be options to circumvent the need to pay the base premium of the plan, subject to employer approval. Any person who meets the definition of a dependent of the insured employee under Section 152 of the

Internal Revenue Code and is covered as a dependent under the base health plan typically qualifies. Each person enrolled in the plan must usually be covered by a qualifying base health plan; the plan is compatible with almost all fully insured and self-funded medical reimbursement plans—even high deductible health plans.

Many businesses use supplemental insurance plans like these to provide benefits to owners, partners, sole proprietors, members of LLCs, and the highly compensated employees of regular corporations. These plans are especially beneficial when a key person or owner is not allowed to participate in employer-sponsored 125 Plans or health reimbursement arrangements. With a supplemental insurance plan, it may be that everyone saves.

Through the use of specialized programs and products, as well as careful and creative planning, you too can stop bleeding cash on your healthcare expenses.

CHAPTER SIX
Stop Bleeding Cash
on Your Life Insurance Premiums

Most people love having life insurance, but hate paying for it. Who wants to pay for something they are absolutely guaranteed not to be able to enjoy themselves? In my opinion, it is just one of those necessary evils. Therefore, the normal course of action for many people is to go cheap and buy the lowest-cost term insurance policy they can find, and hope they never have to use it. The problem here is that most people don't know how to use a value equation in life insurance planning. They also fail to find the right type of leverage to acquire the policy.

Life insurance is always a difficult choice. For me, it would appear that the insurance industry has spent countless dollars to avoid making it any simpler. They offer term insurance with numerous ways to guarantee the cost for as many years as you want—as long as you are willing to pay more to guarantee it for a longer period. If you want permanent insurance, you can buy whole life, universal life, or variable life products, and each variety comes with its own investment component. Are you buying the policy because you made an intelligent and educated decision? The process can be very complicated and troublesome.

While there is no one-size-fits-all solution, I believe it is possible to simplify one piece of information that, if applied correctly, can cut your cost on any product by a substantial margin and offer the potential of tax-favored income in your future.

Please note that the following example provides an over-simplified scenario that may or may not be appropriate for your financial situation. Each product, service, or approach referenced serves a specific purpose with features, risks, and expenses that need to be considered in relation to each client's needs and objectives.

Here is how it worked for two families we work with. Mike and Sheila came to me with a need for a large life insurance policy of over $5,000,000. They had all the money they needed to support their lifestyle, even without their retirement plan assets, which totaled almost $2,000,000. The purpose of the insurance was to provide liquidity for their children in the event that they met an early demise.

Since they did not need it for income, we decided to reformat their retirement plan into a defined contribution plan and place the life insurance within that plan. After carefully considering the risks and benefits as they applied to their unique situation and consulting with tax and legal counsel, the cost of their policies was over $100,000 per year in premiums, but because we used money inside their retirement plan to pay that premium, the cost was essentially cut in half.

It is important to review all the risks and benefits of this possible solution, especially since all premium costs need to be returned to the retirement plan upon the death of the insured.

Please note that the following example provides an over-simplified scenario that may or may not be appropriate for your financial situation. Each product, service, or approach referenced serves a specific purpose with features, risks, and expenses that need to be considered in relation to each client's needs and objectives.

In another example, we have Johnny and Karen, who came to me via their CPA to find a strategy that would allow them to use tax-deductible dollars from their corporation, and it was in excess of what they needed to contribute to their qualified retirement plan.

At first I was at a little bit of a loss for what to do, but after I asked a series of in-depth questions, some unknown facts came to the surface. The first question concerned the value of the business, and who would run the business if Johnny were not able to do it. Karen and Johnny looked at each other with a blank stare. They had considered their children, but jointly came to the conclusion that the kids were too young to take on that kind of responsibility. Then Johnny said that Karen could simply hire someone to take his place. Their business was a fire systems installation company, and they quickly concluded that they could hire individuals to take specific jobs, but they had no one capable enough to run the business functions.

I then asked if Karen would sell the business if Johnny weren't there, and she said that she would probably have to. I explained that her situation would be more like a fire sale, one that would potentially discount the value of the business because there was no guarantee that it would even operate efficiently without Johnny. I suggested that they use the extra money the company was earning to buy a life insurance policy that would buy enough time to find the right buyer. They seemed to like the idea, but only if they could gain some tax leverage on the purchase. I said that I knew of some strategies, but nothing that was completely black and white, and that I would do the research.

I found a plan called a Section 79 Group Life Insurance Purchase plan, which would allow Johnny to acquire a group term life insurance plan with up to $50,000 of coverage on all eligible employees in a fully tax-deductible payment. They liked it, but said that was not enough coverage, $50,000 just doesn't go very far in today's world. I advised them to sit tight and listen while I told them how to leverage large sums in this plan with a slight twist. The next step was to offer all employees the ability to purchase additional coverage—at company expense—if they were willing to pay the tax on the income used to purchase it. Since most employees won't see the value and would have to pay taxes on the money, they could stick with just the free $50,000 policy and waive the rest. Johnny and Karen (who also was on payroll) could both opt in and take the coverage, which was also available in a permanent product, as long as they would accept the economic benefit (income at a discount) on their tax documents (W-2) at the end of the year.

They loved it and took it. Johnny had coverage for Karen at $1,000,000, which he had never had before, and Karen had $450,000 of permanent coverage for Johnny. They both needed it so they would be able to take care of any financial needs for the kids, who were still in school. So, all in all, they got almost everything they wanted: coverage for the family and protection for the business, and a large discount on the premium from the income tax application.

But, unfortunately, the story didn't end there. About a year after they took out the Section 79 based life insurance policies, Karen got into a car accident on her way home from work and died on the spot. Johnny lost a lot of time at work due to stress and circumstance. If not for the $450,000 death benefit (not even on the principal of the company), much more would have been lost. More evidence of the value of proper planning.

There are possible ways to defer or eliminate the actual premium expense of a life insurance policy that include specific risks. Many people, including small business owners, have two things in common in their business: A life insurance policy for family or business, and a retirement plan that their advisors made sure they entered into. If you have an expense that you know you have to pay, and you have retirement plans that can pay it for you, it may be possible to use the deductible dollars of a retirement plan to pay that expense if you understand the risks of doing so.

There are other possible considerations, depending on each individual's unique circumstances. What if you want to make your life insurance look, smell, and taste like an investment? I call this investment grade life insurance. (Please note that Investment Grade Life Insurance is a term coined by the author. An Investment Grade Life Insurance policy is formed by utilizing an existing Indexed Universal Life product from any accepting carrier and making a single premium payment to the policy. The formation of Investment Grade Life Insurance initiates a Modified Endowment Contract by current insurance code federally. This could have a negative impact on your taxes, especially if you are under the age of 59½, and could incur tax penalties. Please consult your tax advisor for your specific needs. Also, policy loans may have a ceiling and a floor rate and carrier rules vary. Policies studied herein have loan rates based upon the Moody's bond index with a guaranteed ceiling rate of 5 to 5.3%. Index returns vary annually. Please refer to your policy for specifics.) You can place that in the retirement plan and have a more conservative investment, but in the event of early death, it turns into a life insurance policy. If you get to retirement, you can use the policy for income, just like a retirement plan.

The last way to possibly leverage the cost of your life insurance is incredibly simple, yet so few people do it. Let's assume that you have savings inside an annuity, or maybe even in a bank account. You are getting little or no rate of return on the bank savings, and the annuity is very conservative as well. These are your emergency dollars. If you make a single premium payment to an investment grade policy, you could increase the potential rate of return without necessarily increasing the risk. If you do this, not only could you get an added rate of return, you could also possibly get higher liquidity than the annuity, and in the event of death, you could convert all of your earnings into tax-free capital via the death benefit.

In my opinion, a life insurance policy may be one of the best places to hold your safe money, either for a business or in your personal life. The loan on the policy is not to carry or trade securities; it is intended to state that the policy loan can be used for borrowing purposes other than—or less expensive than—loans from traditional resources, such as banks or credit cards.

These are just a few ways to maximize your money, increase your spendability, and stop bleeding cash on your life insurance premiums!

Take the Next Step!

If, after reading this book, you feel these creative solutions can work to help you stop bleeding cash, it would be my pleasure to offer you a complementary consultation and assessment. After I give you the assessment, you can decide whether we proceed together. If you have an "A-ha!" moment, it may be time to look at some out-of-the-box solutions! What I mean by an "A-ha" moment is when that little light bulb goes off in your head, telling you something that can refocus your thought process—something you had not thought of before. We often hear the phrase, "Why didn't my advisor tell me that?" Or "I've never quite seen it explained that simply!"

And just remember this: the cost of this book, and the time you have invested in reading it, will potentially benefit you in many ways and start you toward your financial destination. My peers charge their fees just for plan design, and I always ask them why. The answer might surprise you! Most frequently it is because if the client doesn't like their solutions, at least they get paid for their time.

Personally, I believe in results-oriented planning. If the desired results are not achieved, is that something that my clients should pay for? If you go to a restaurant, and the food is bad, do you have to pay for it? The answer is, if the restaurant ever wants you back, they had better not charge you for something unsatisfactory. I was taught early in my career that there are only two things you need to succeed: The first is to obtain clients. That is fairly easy. The second and most critical thing you need is to keep those clients. That takes dedication and work.

If you are interested in receiving any of Barry's free reports entitled "ELFS" Or "Eliminating Losing Financial Strategies" or a complementary consultation direct with Barry, you can call anytime toll free at 1-800-341-5433, e-mail me at bwaxler@ barrywaxler.com, or visit www.barrywaxler.com/ and fill out a contact form. Together, we'll look for the creative solutions that will help you Stop Bleeding Cash!

Visit Barry's YouTube Channel,
Close Up on San Diego Business,
for featured business interviews.

Additional About the Author

Waxler's approach is collaborative; he works with clients' agents, planners, and tax and legal professionals to advise clients on strategic investment platforms that promote wealth accumulation and tax advantages. Waxler focuses on providing long-term, compassionate financial relationships with clients to help them protect their real estate, home equity, and ownership, and avoid significant monetary loss during retirement. In the course of his career he has earned numerous industry sales awards.

Barry lives in San Diego with his children, Kari and Shane, and is on the community Board of Directors for The Disabled Business Persons' Association, and Challenged America. He enjoys the radio, and is the host of a local San Diego radio show, *Close Up On San Diego Business.* On the show, he gets up close and personal with local businesses and other individuals who are making a difference in San Diego.

CPSIA information can be obtained
at www.ICGtesting.com
Printed in the USA
FSOW02n0615130715
8767FS